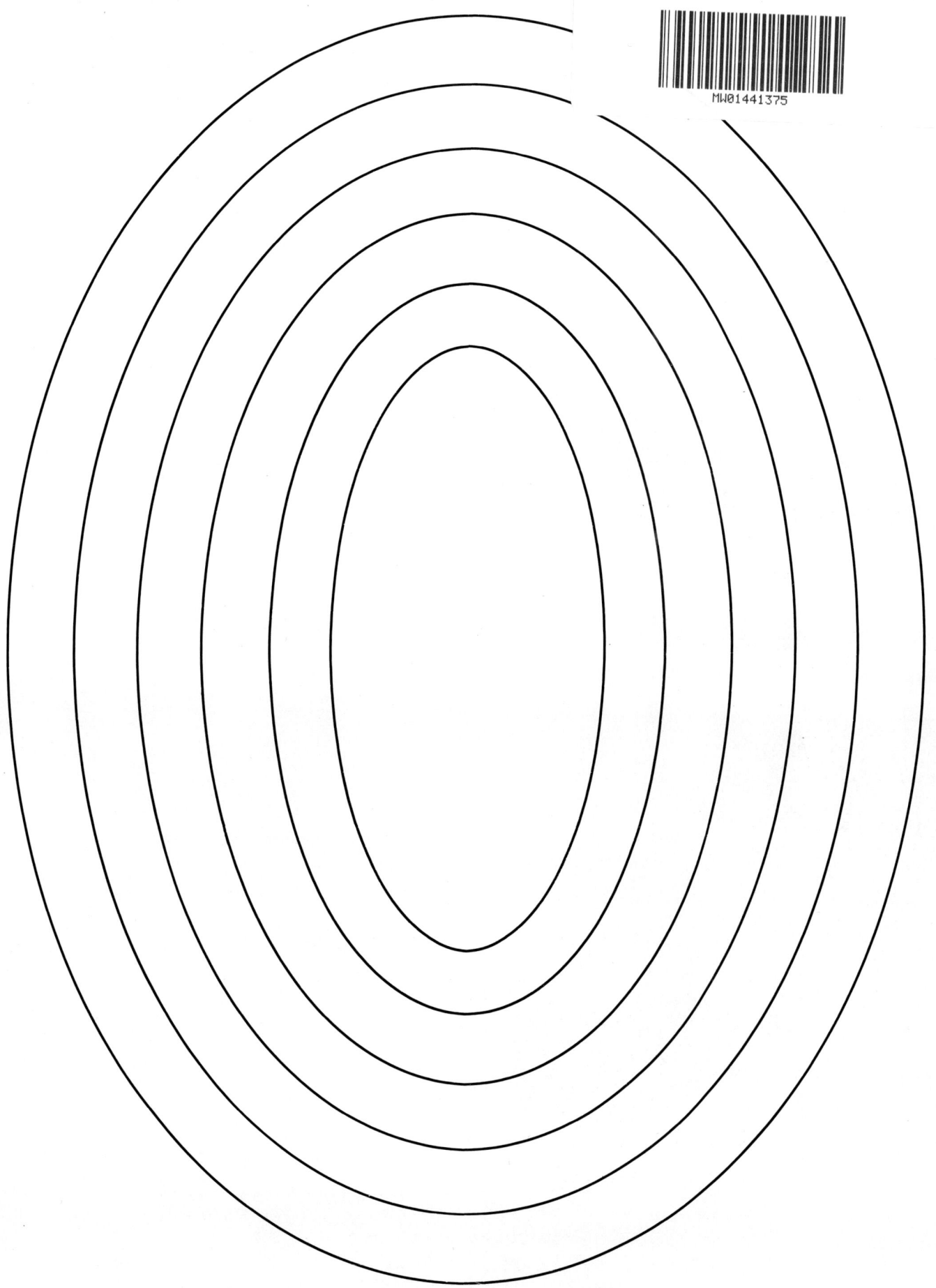

The ovals on plates 1–13 can be nested.

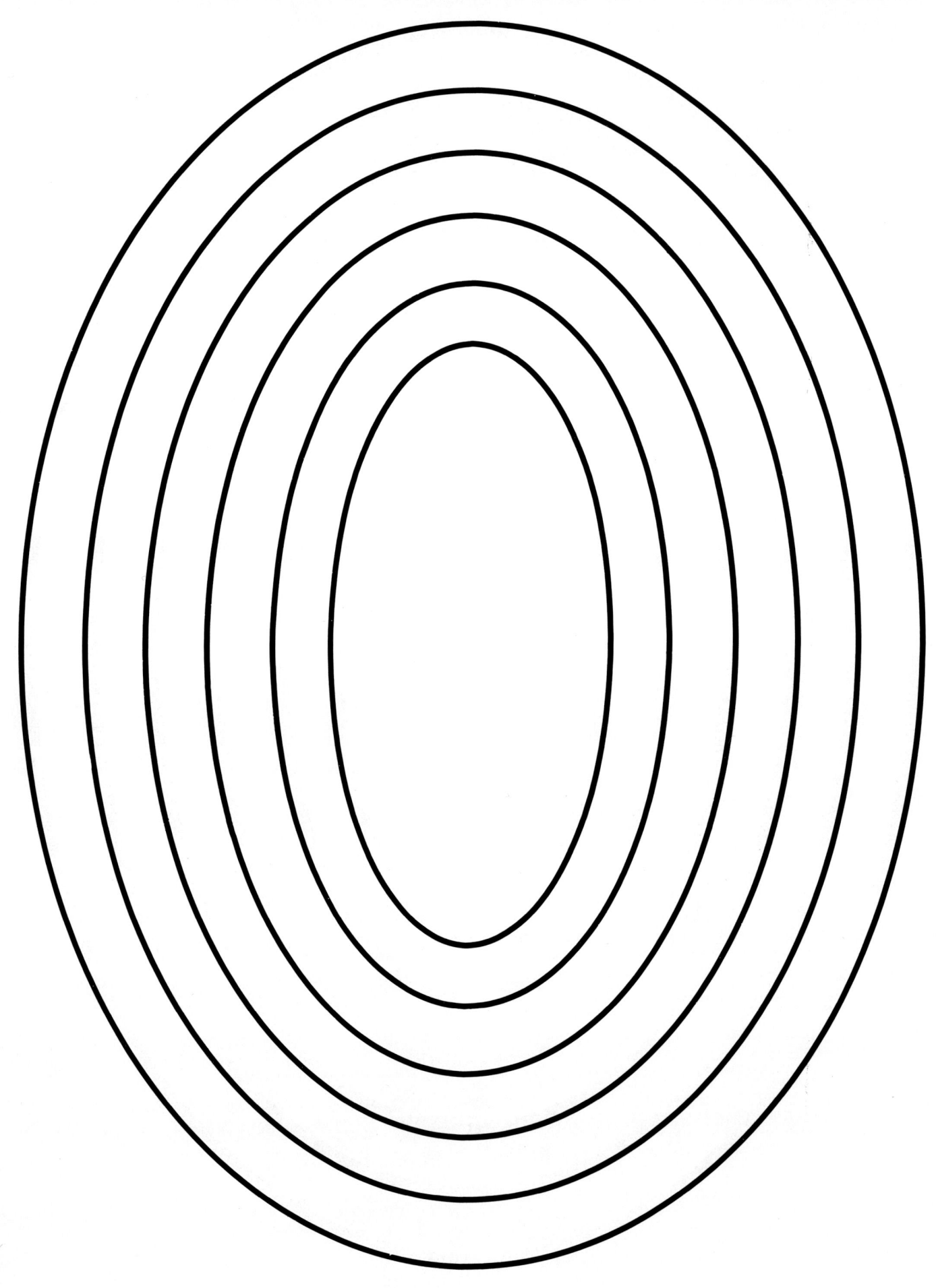

The ovals on plates 1–13 can be nested.

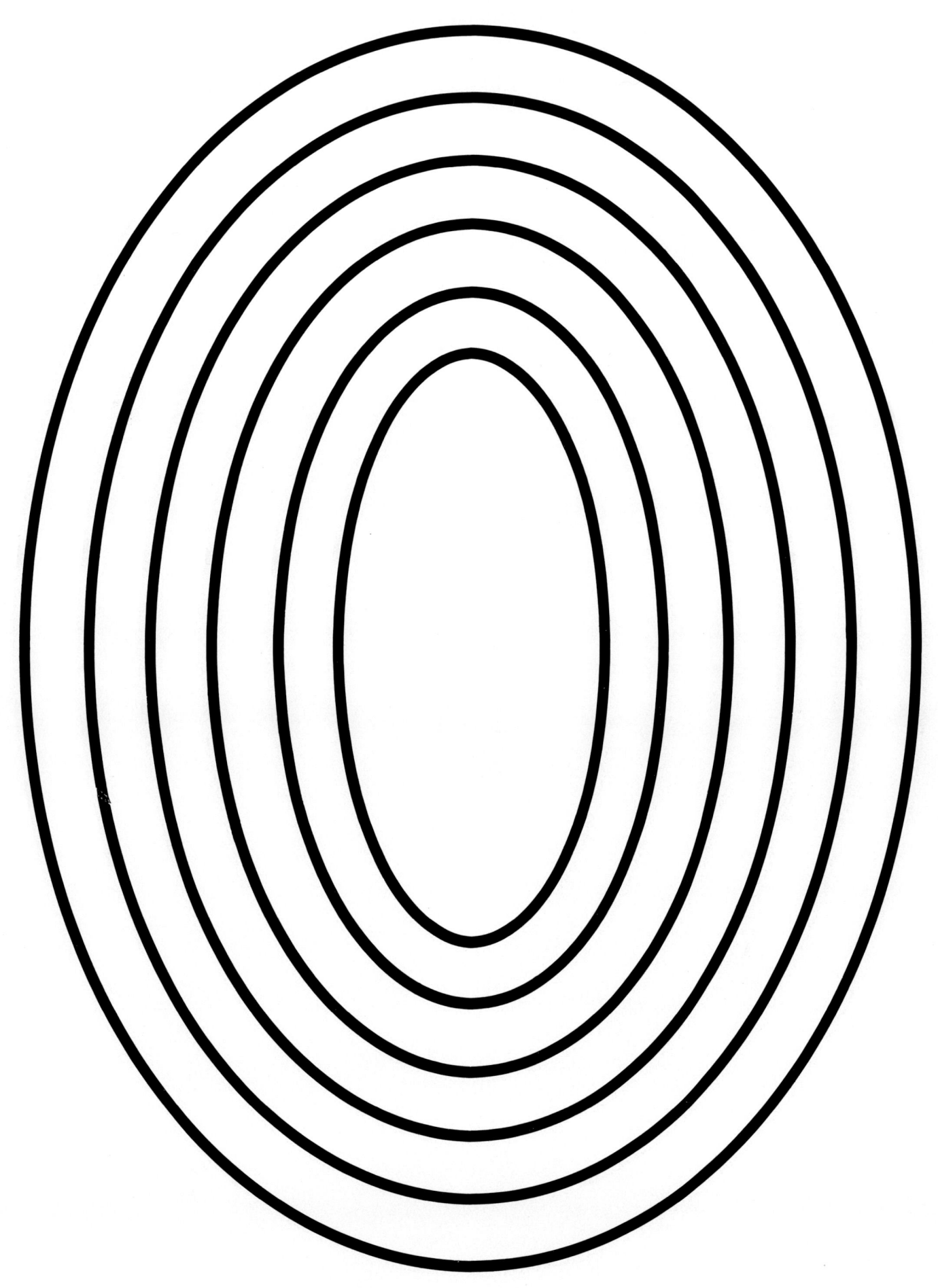

The ovals on plates 1–13 can be nested.

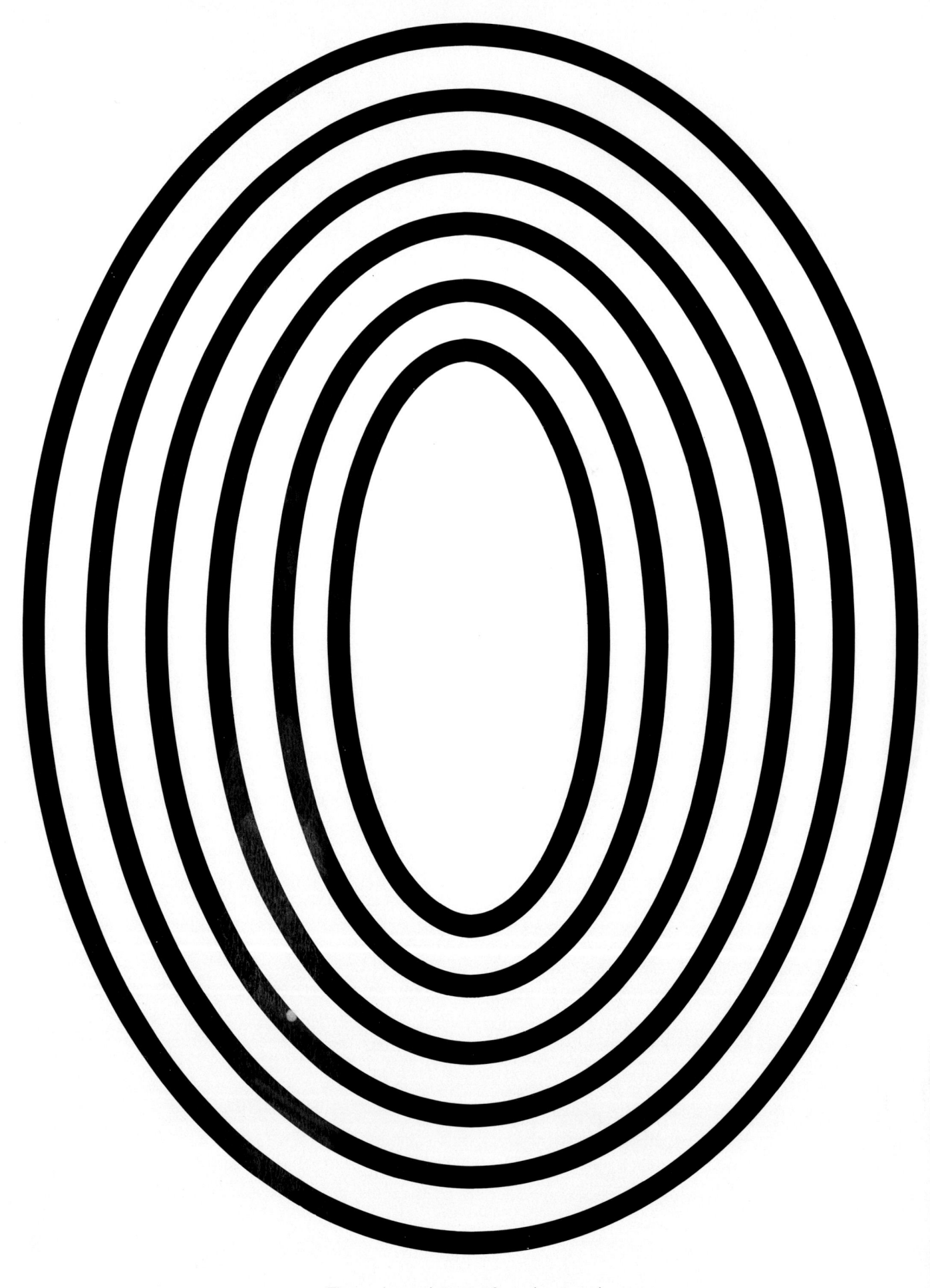

The ovals on plates 1–13 can be nested.

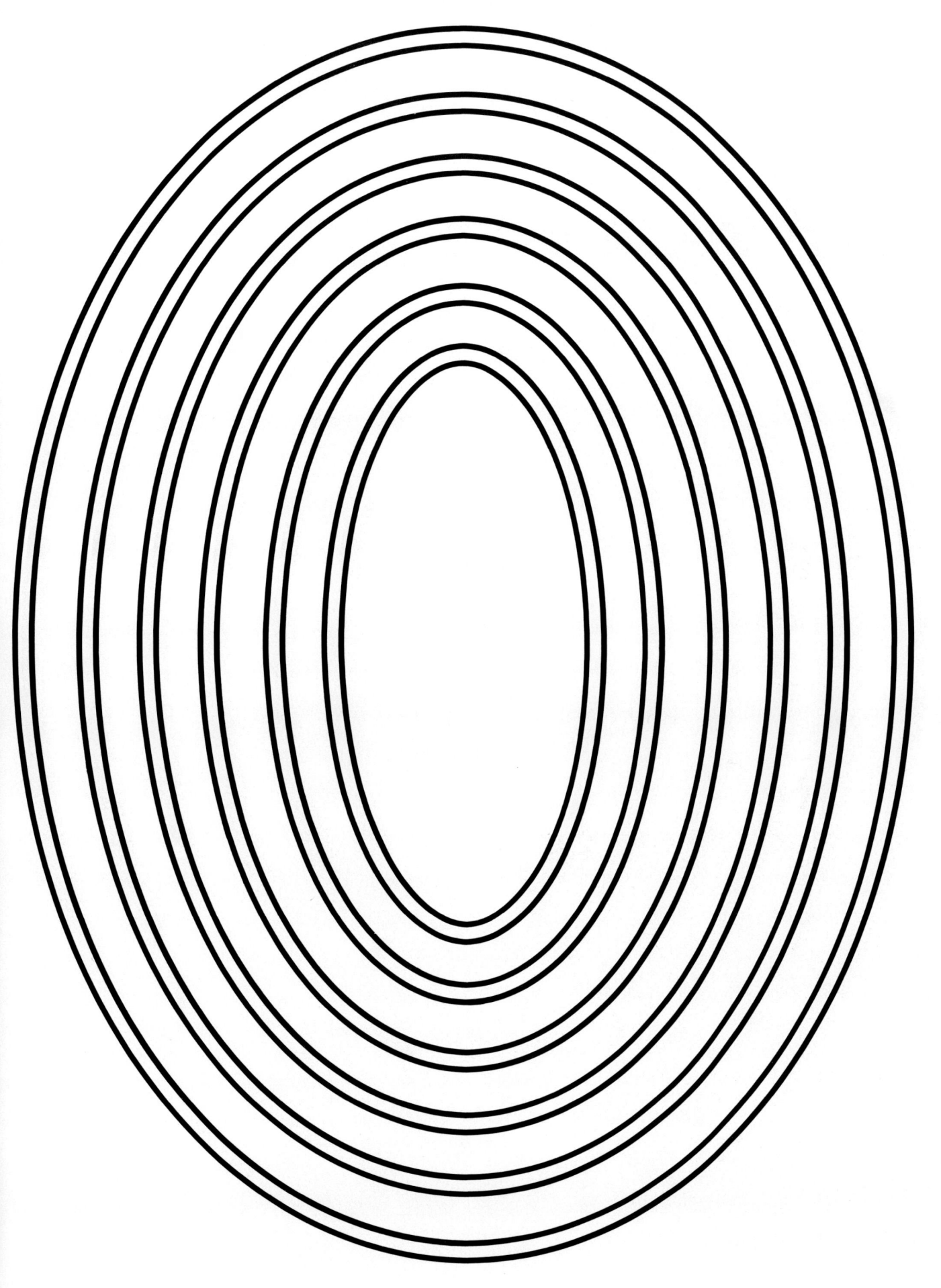
The ovals on plates 1–13 can be nested.

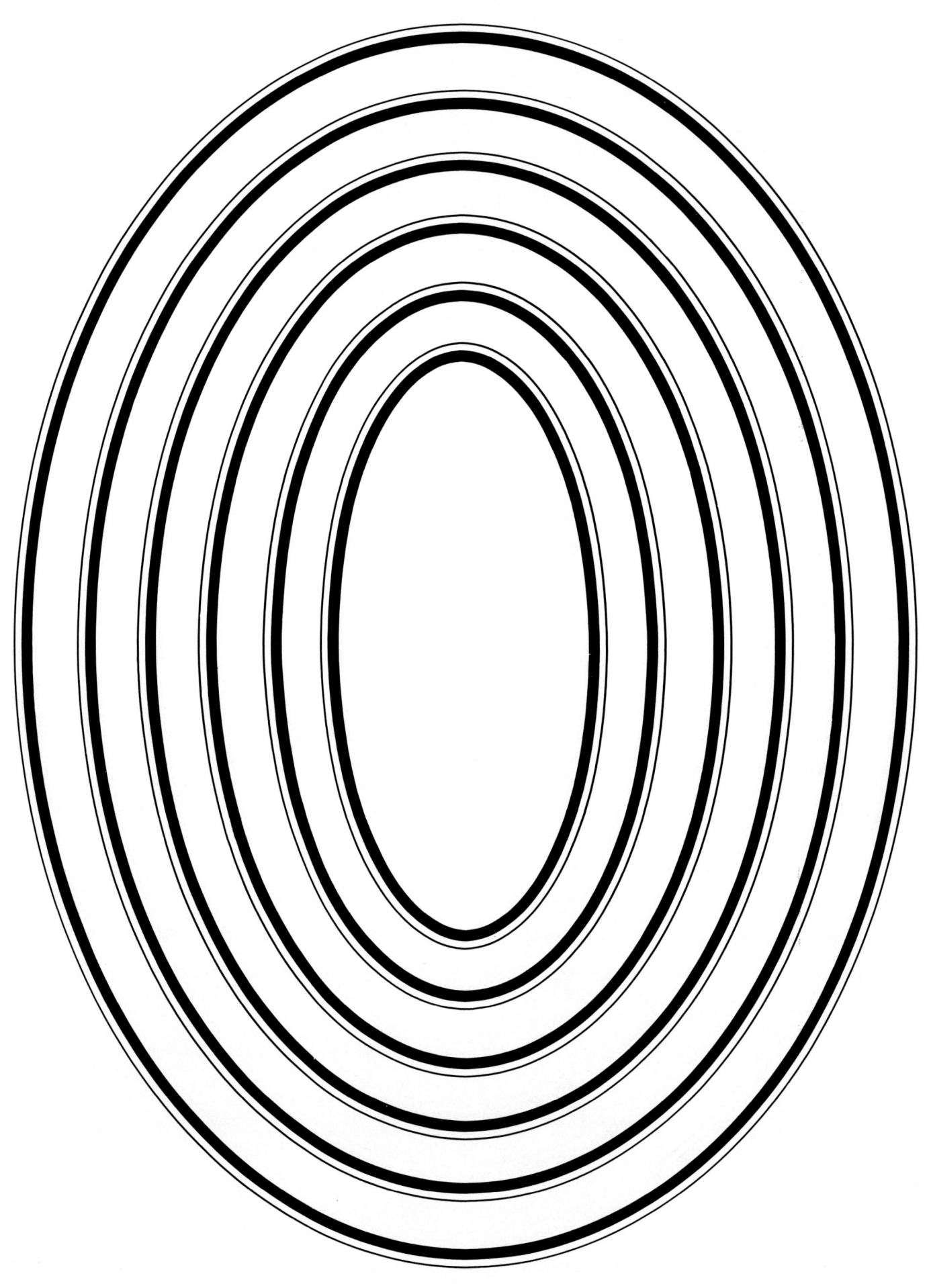

The ovals on plates 1–13 can be nested.

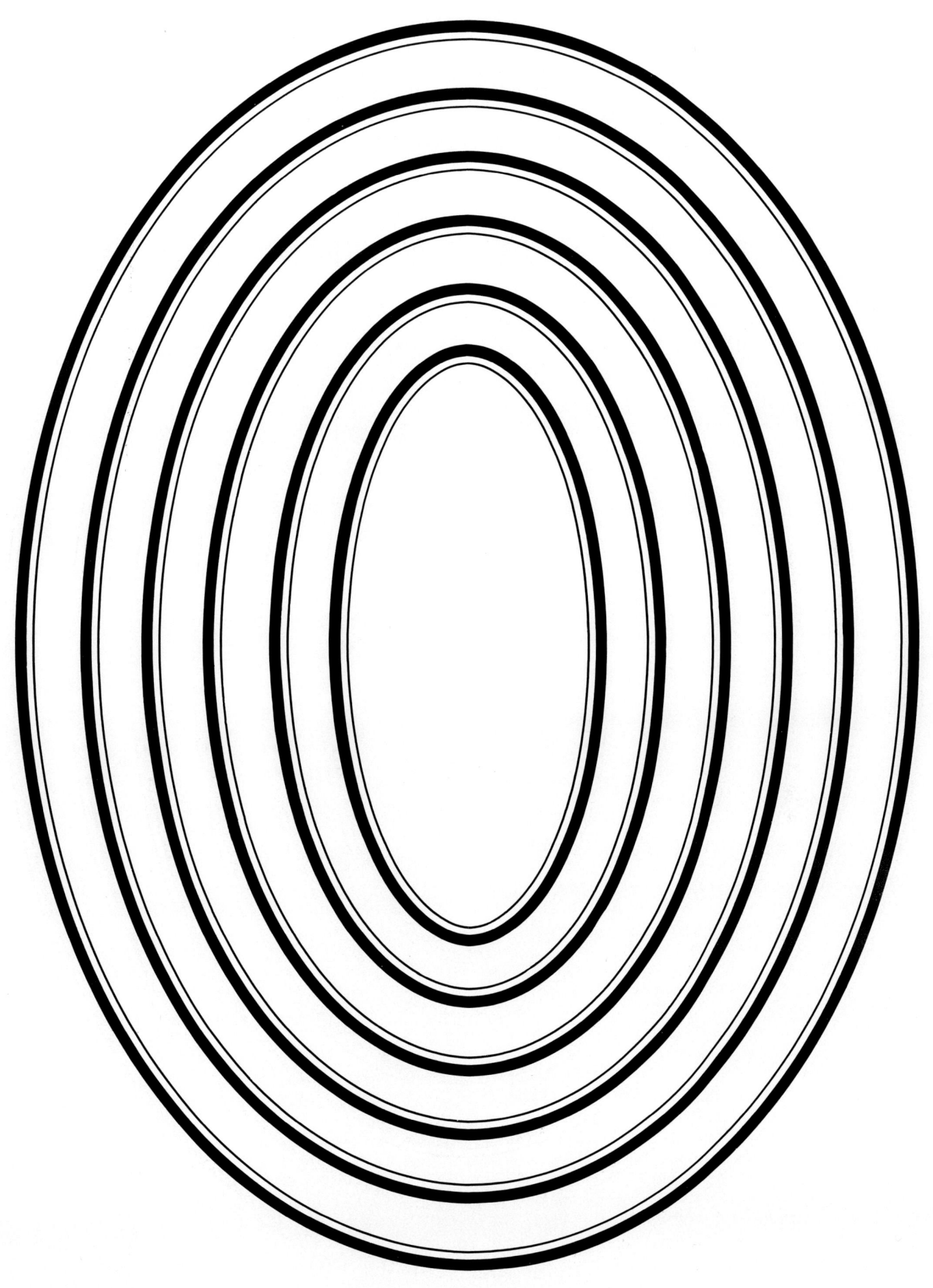

The ovals on plates 1–13 can be nested.

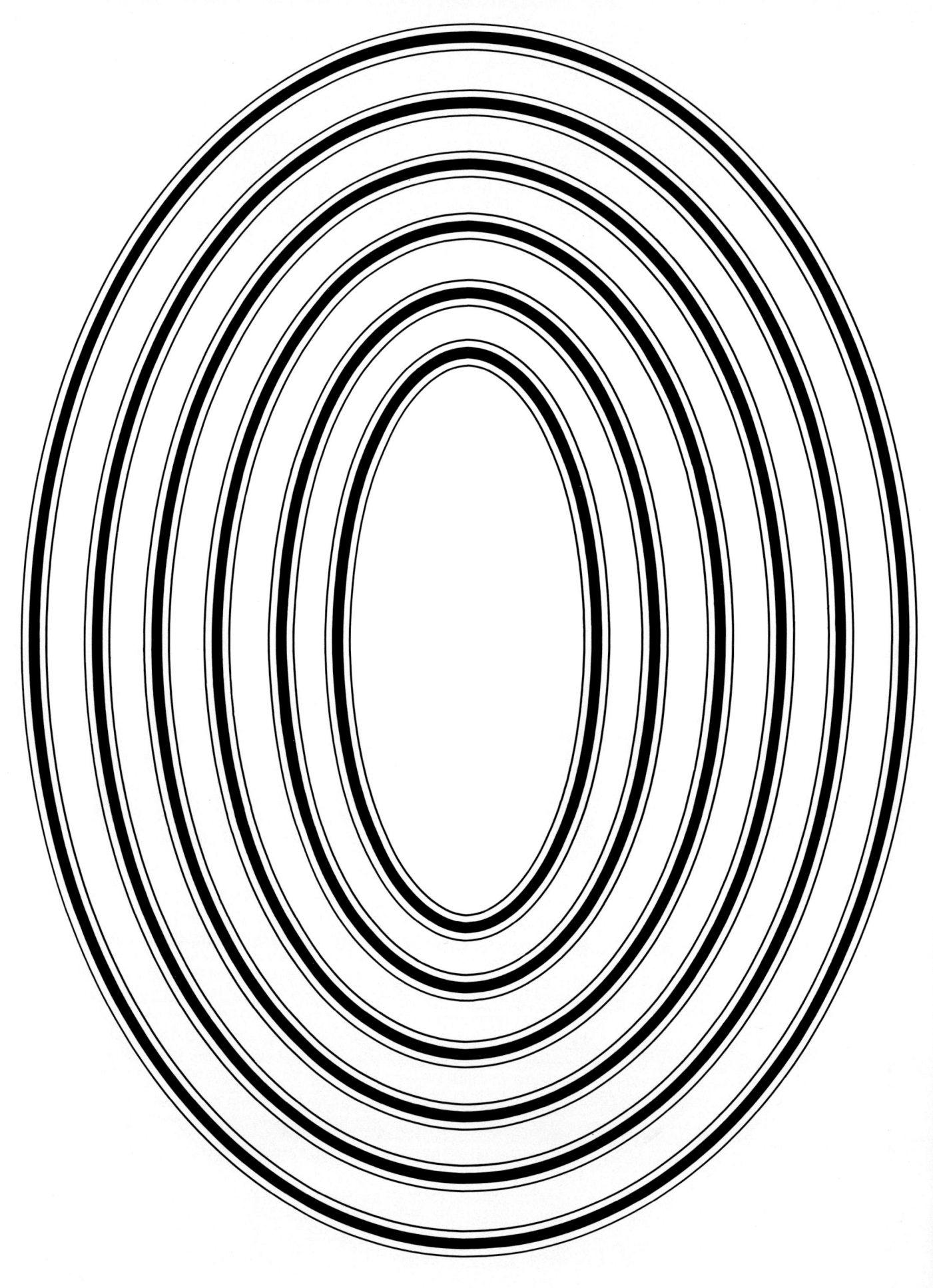

The ovals on plates 1–13 can be nested.

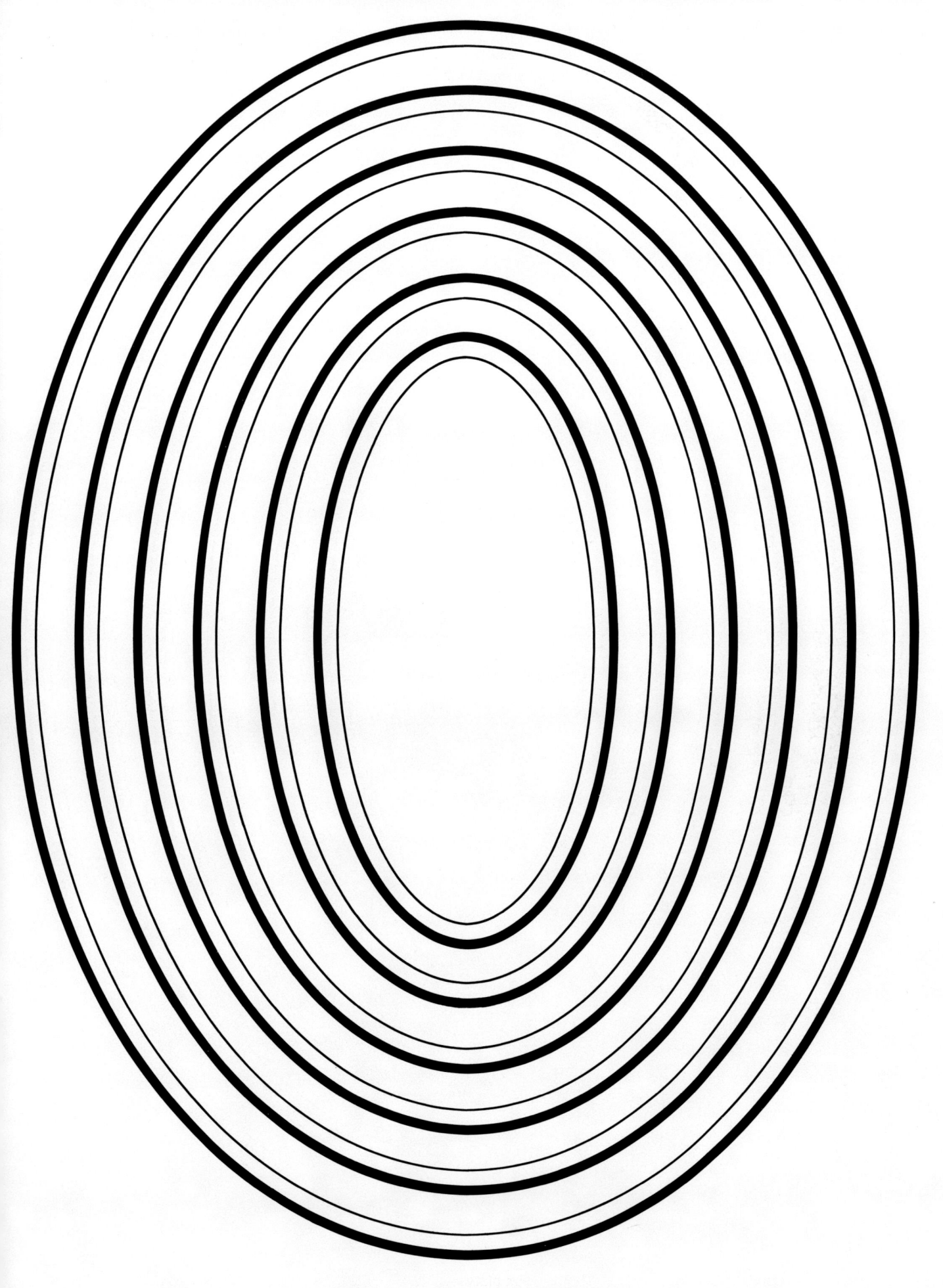

The ovals on plates 1–13 can be nested.

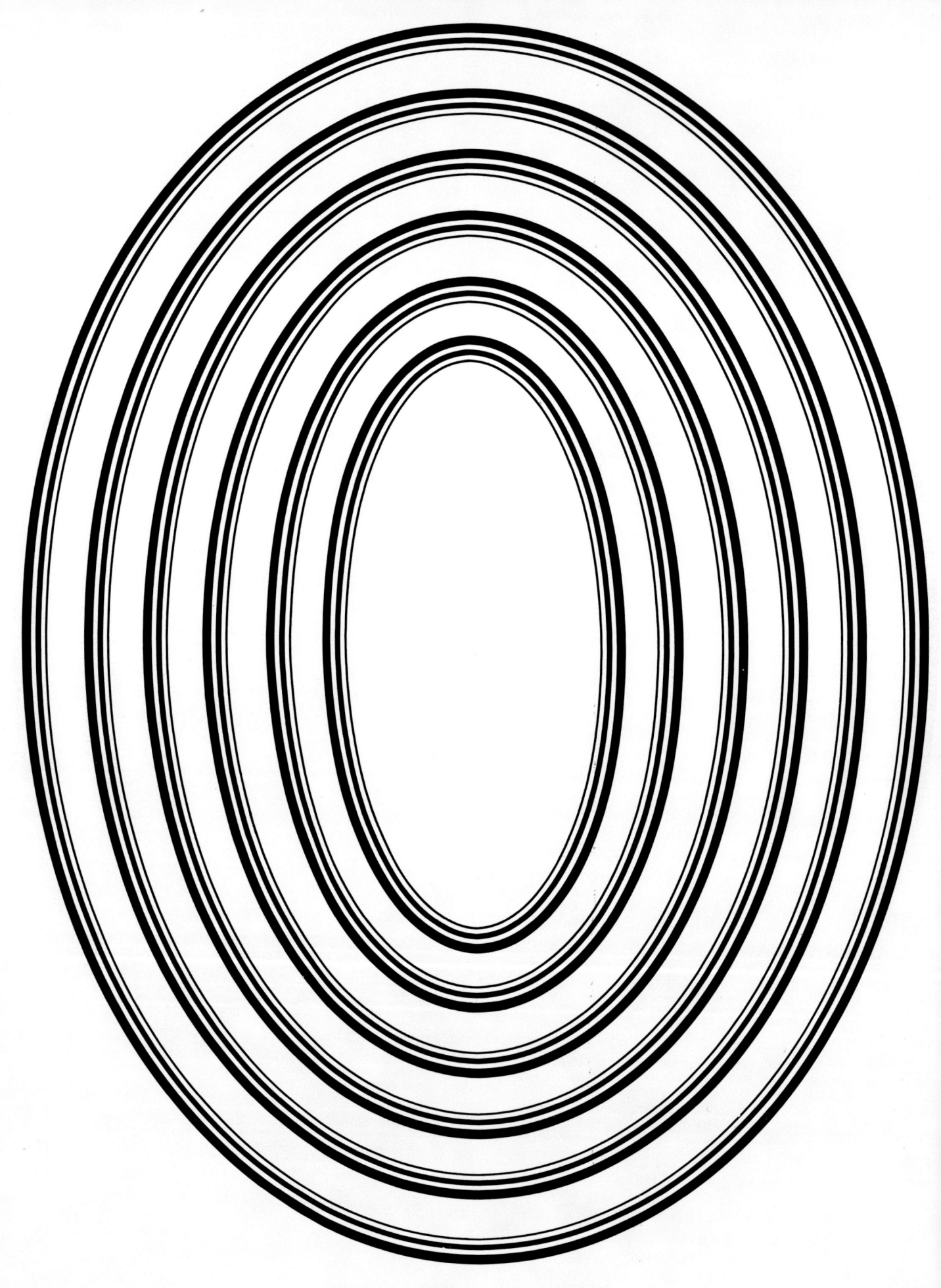
The ovals on plates 1–13 can be nested.

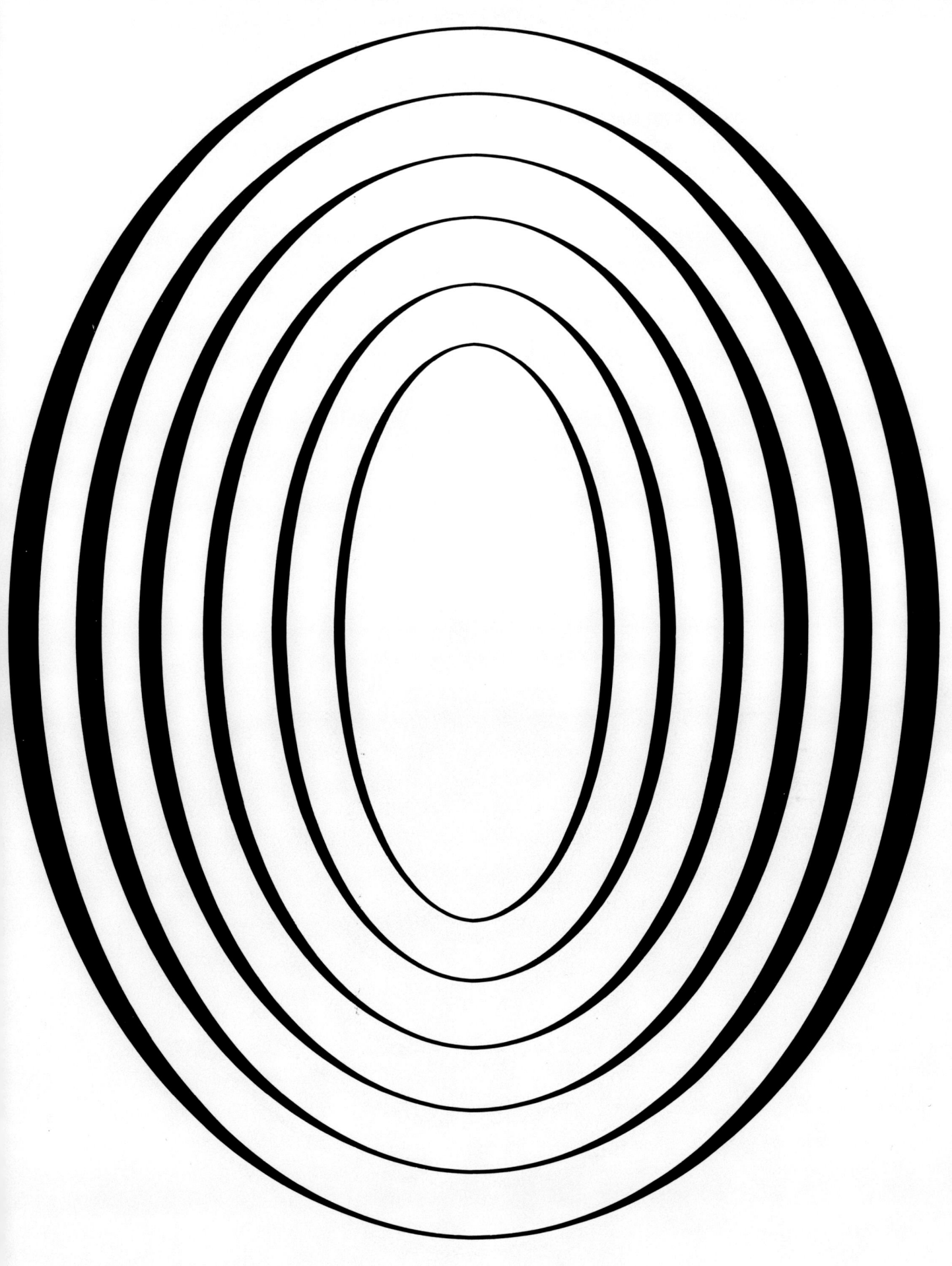

The ovals on plates 1–13 can be nested.

The ovals on plates 1–13 can be nested.

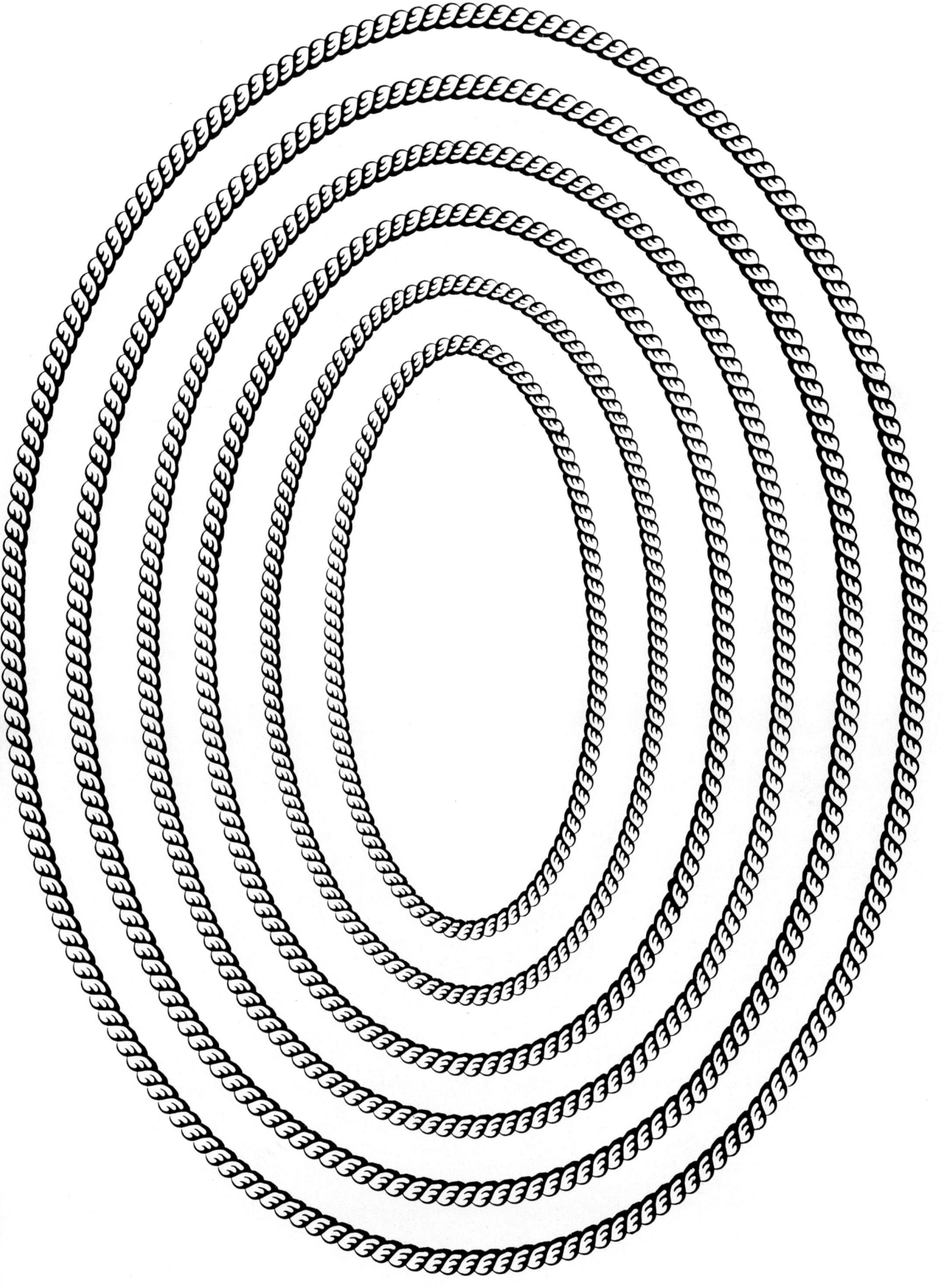

The ovals on plates 1–13 can be nested.

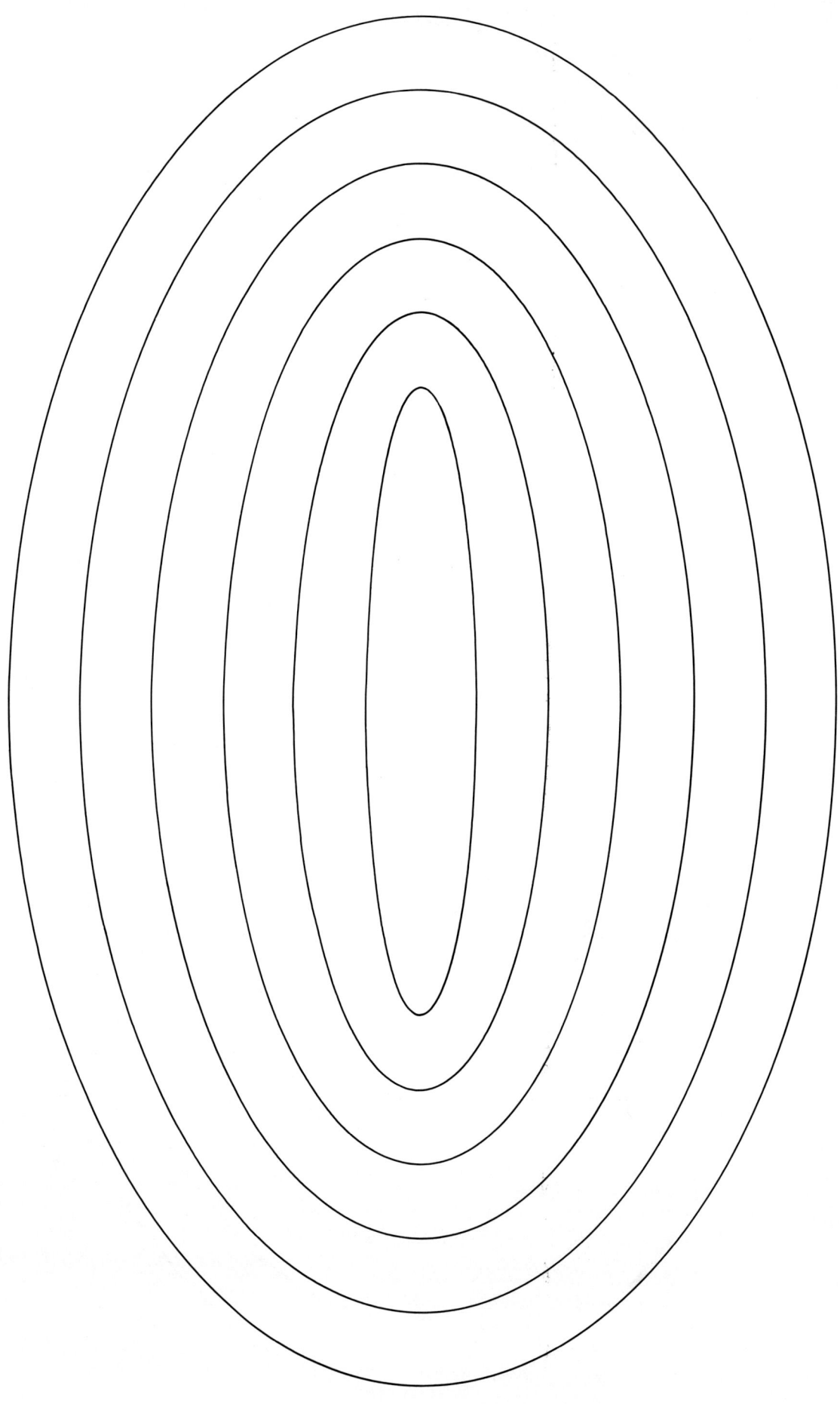

The ovals on plates 14–26 can be nested.

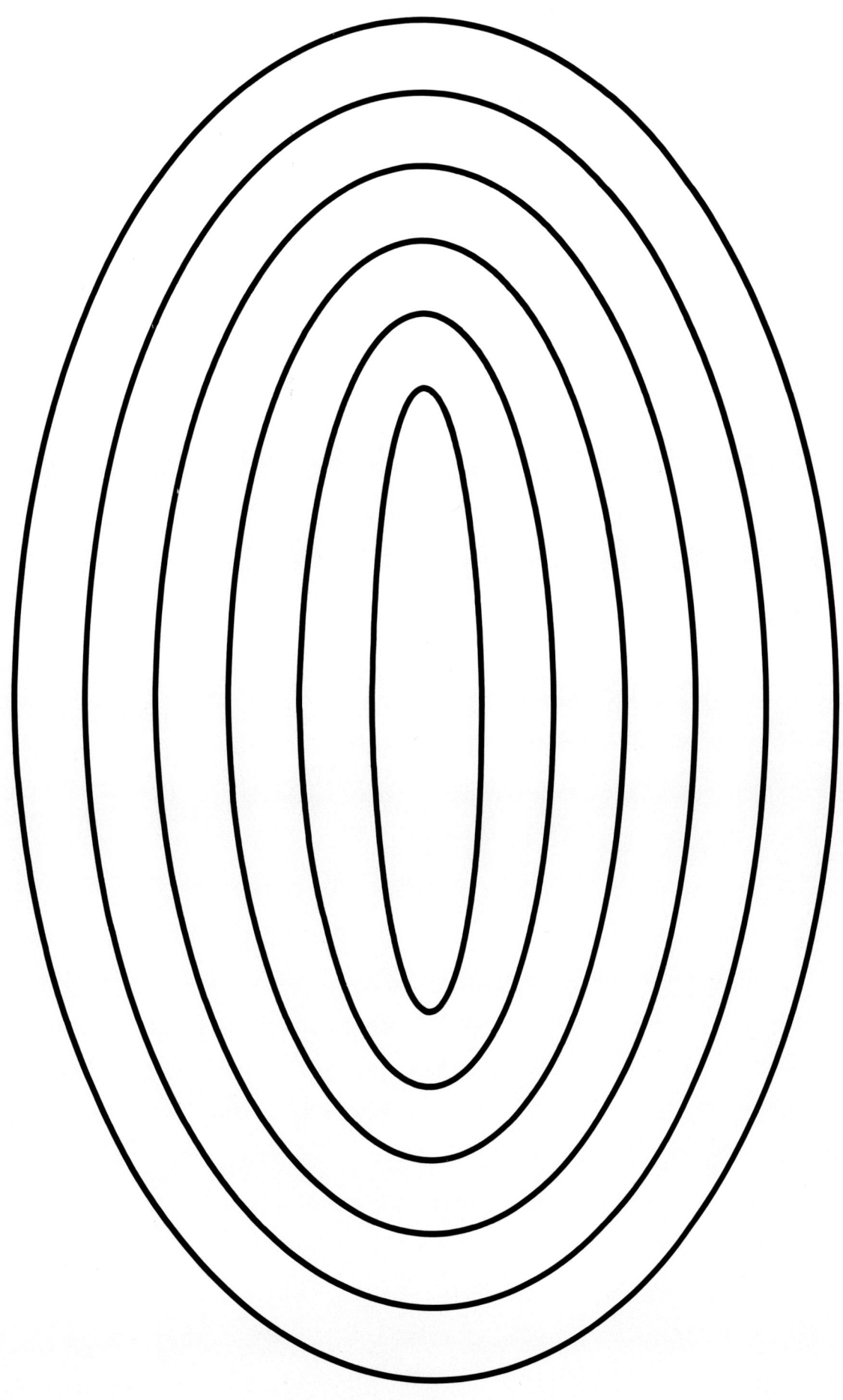

The ovals on plates 14–26 can be nested.

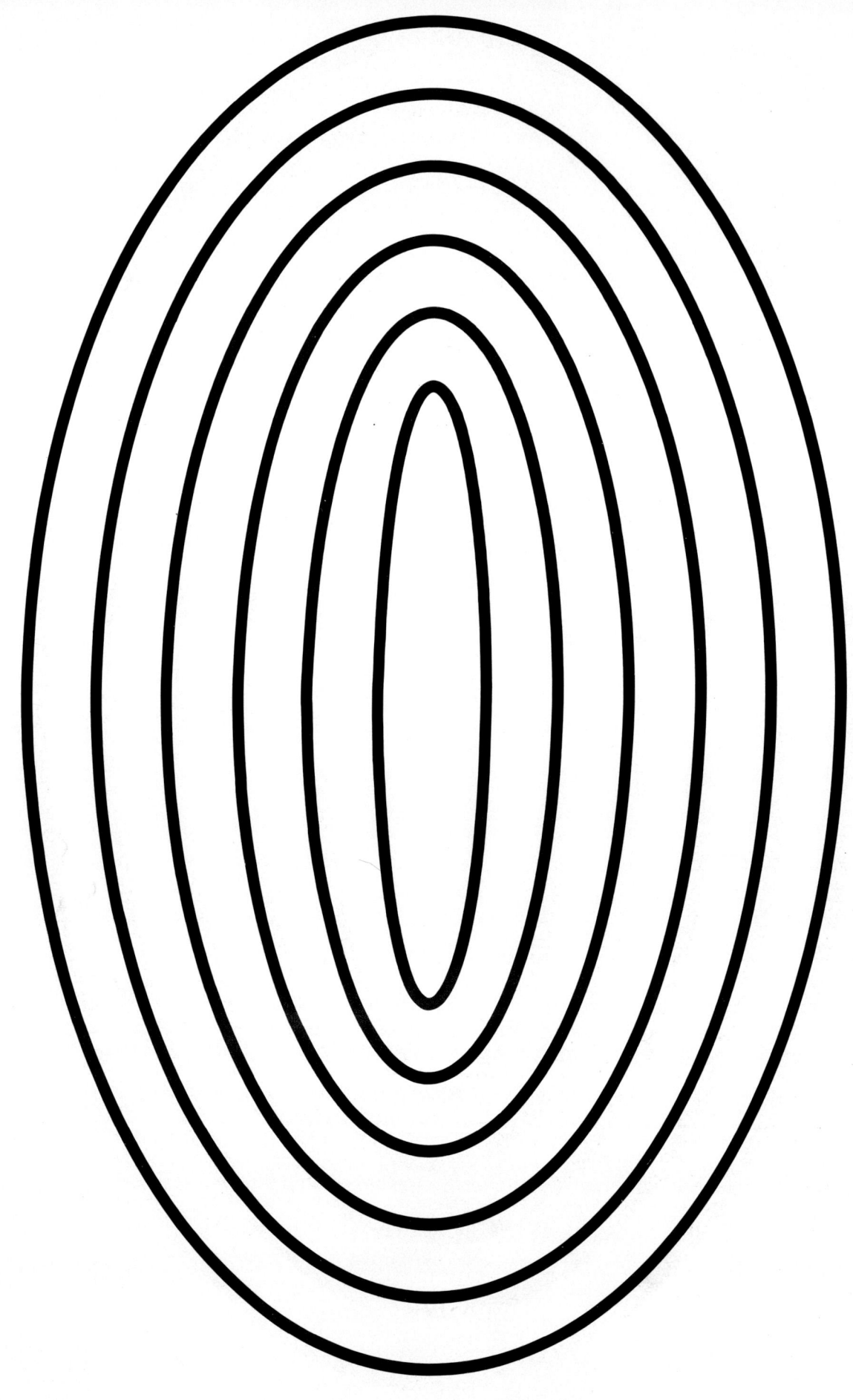

The ovals on plates 14–26 can be nested.

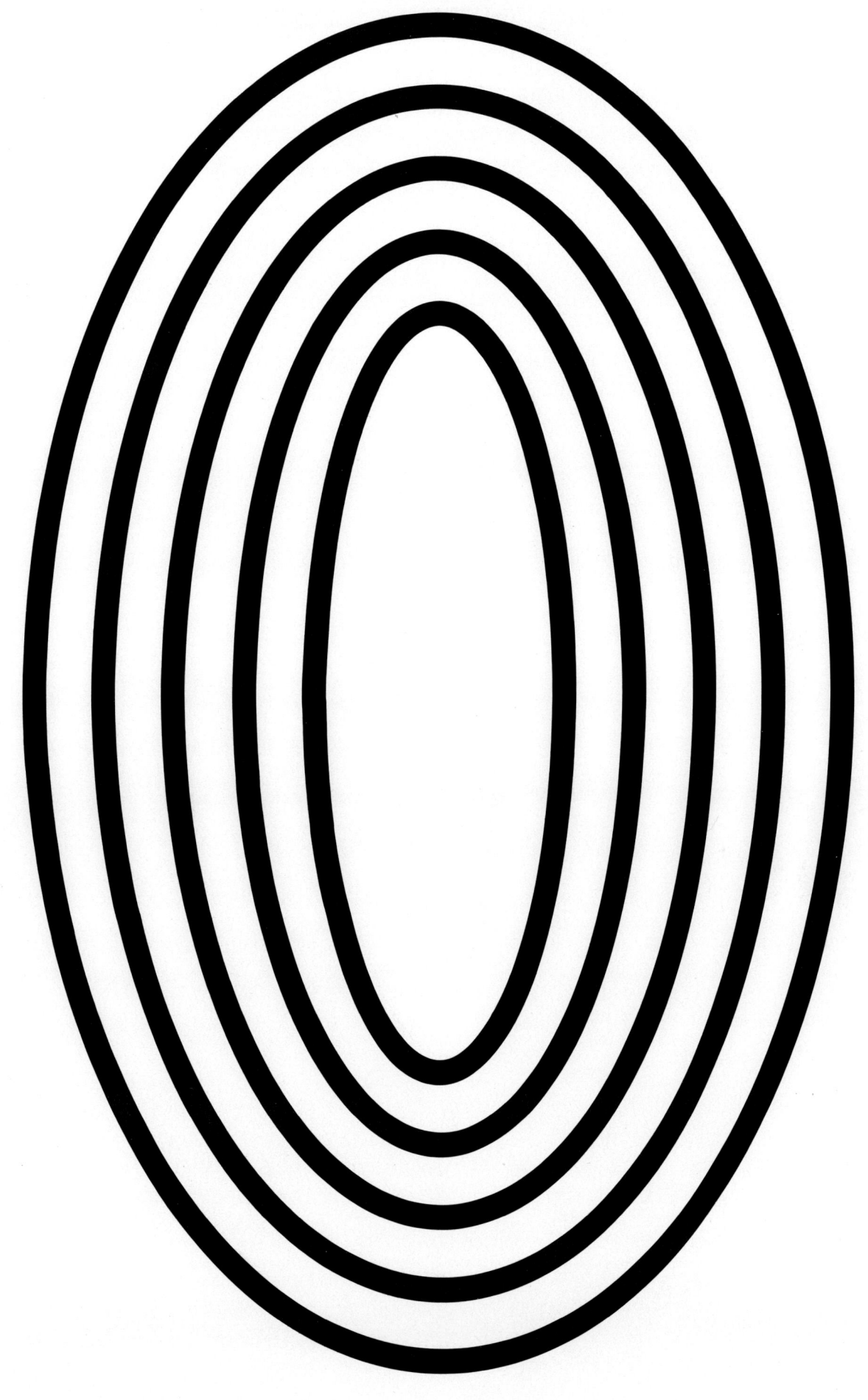

The ovals on plates 14–26 can be nested.

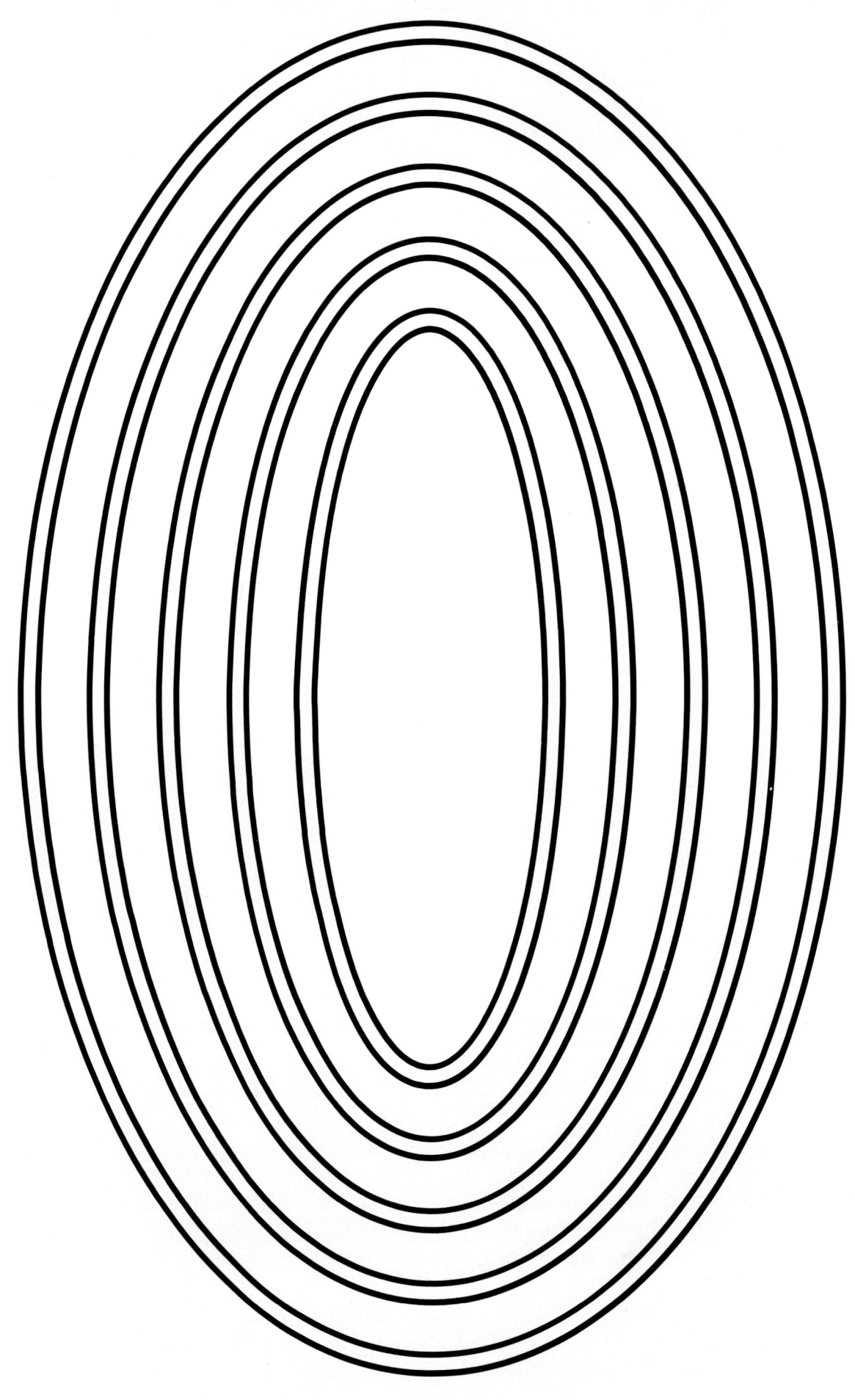

The ovals on plates 14–26 can be nested.

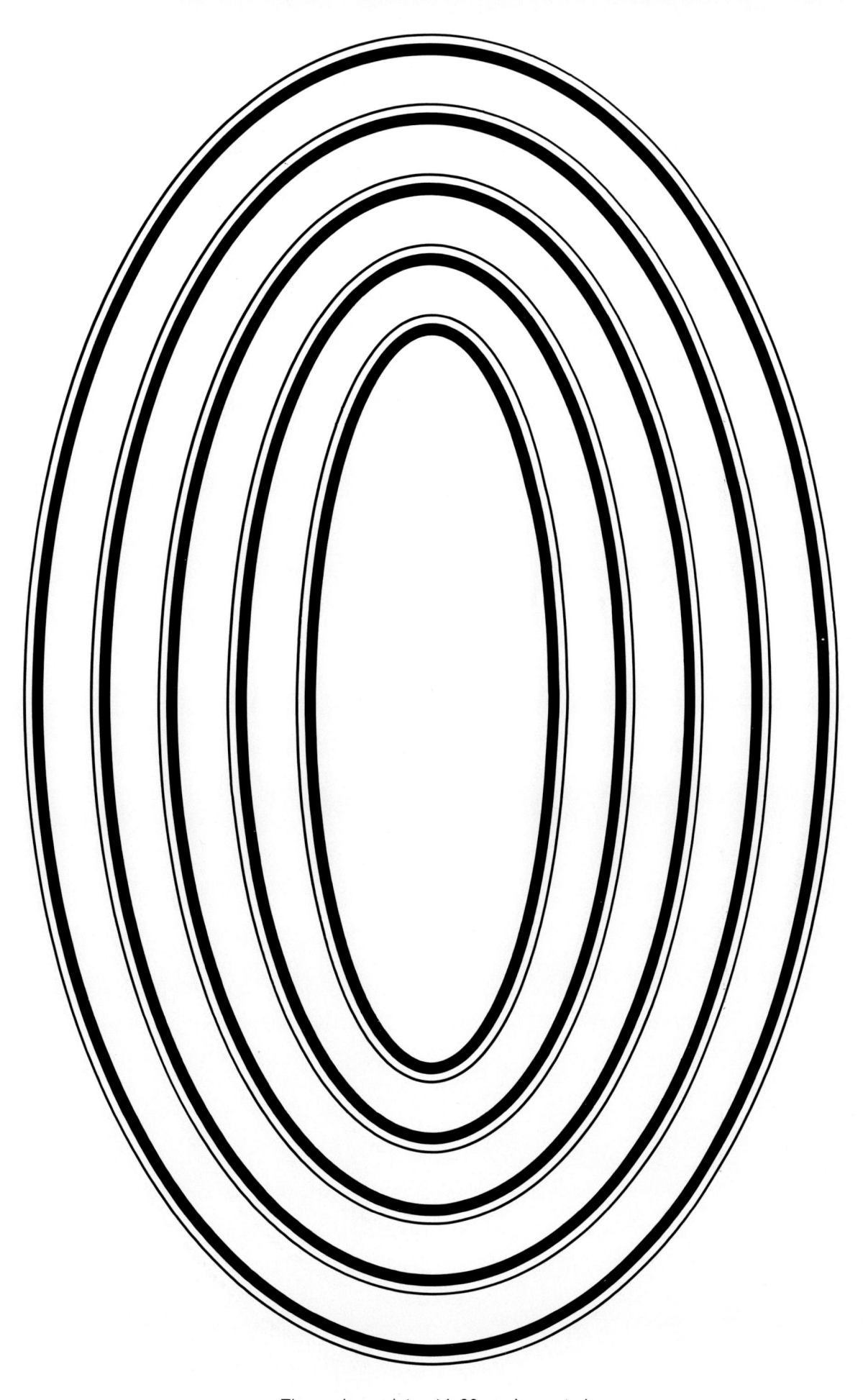

The ovals on plates 14–26 can be nested.

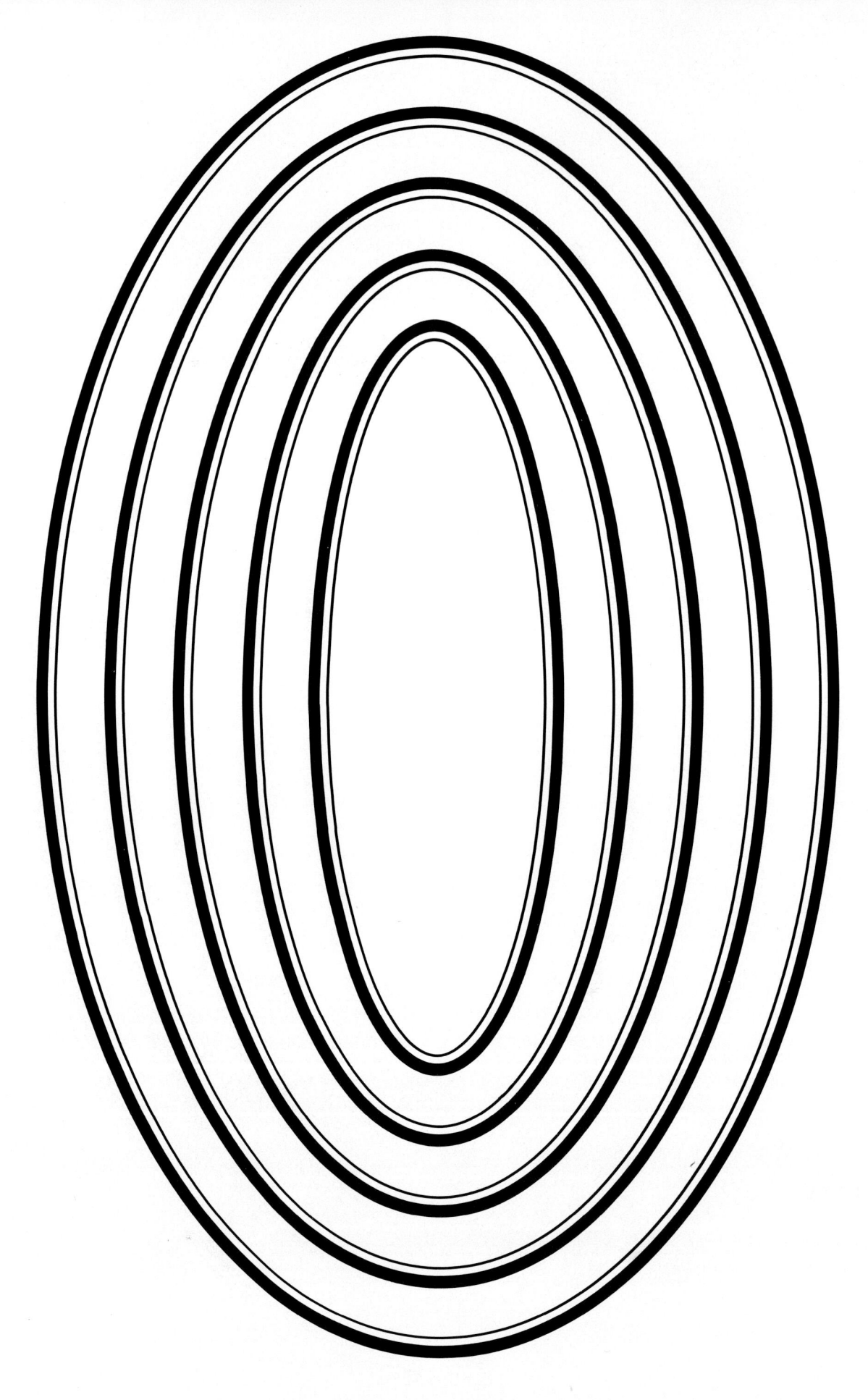

The ovals on plates 14–26 can be nested.

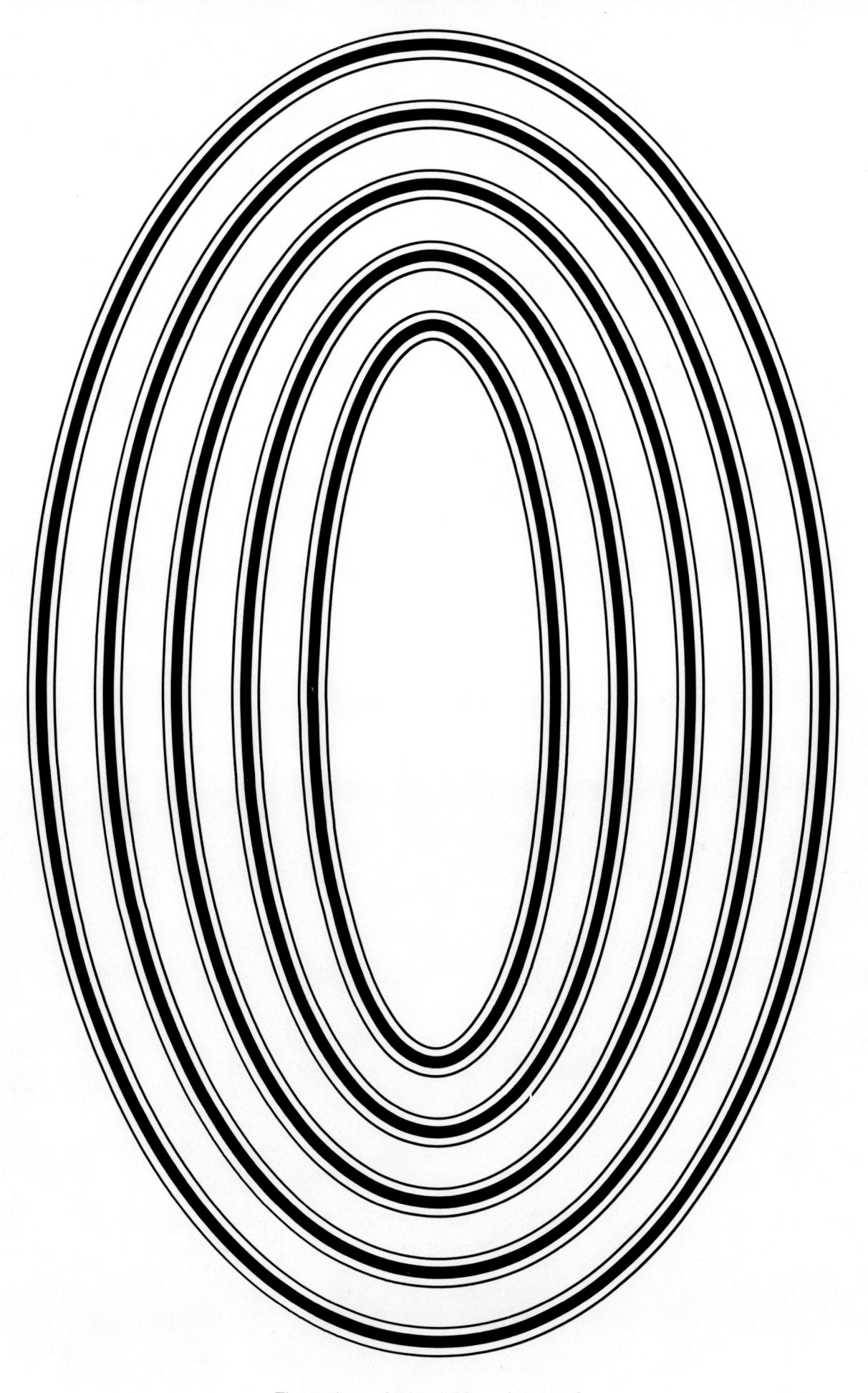

The ovals on plates 14–26 can be nested.

The ovals on plates 1–96 can be used

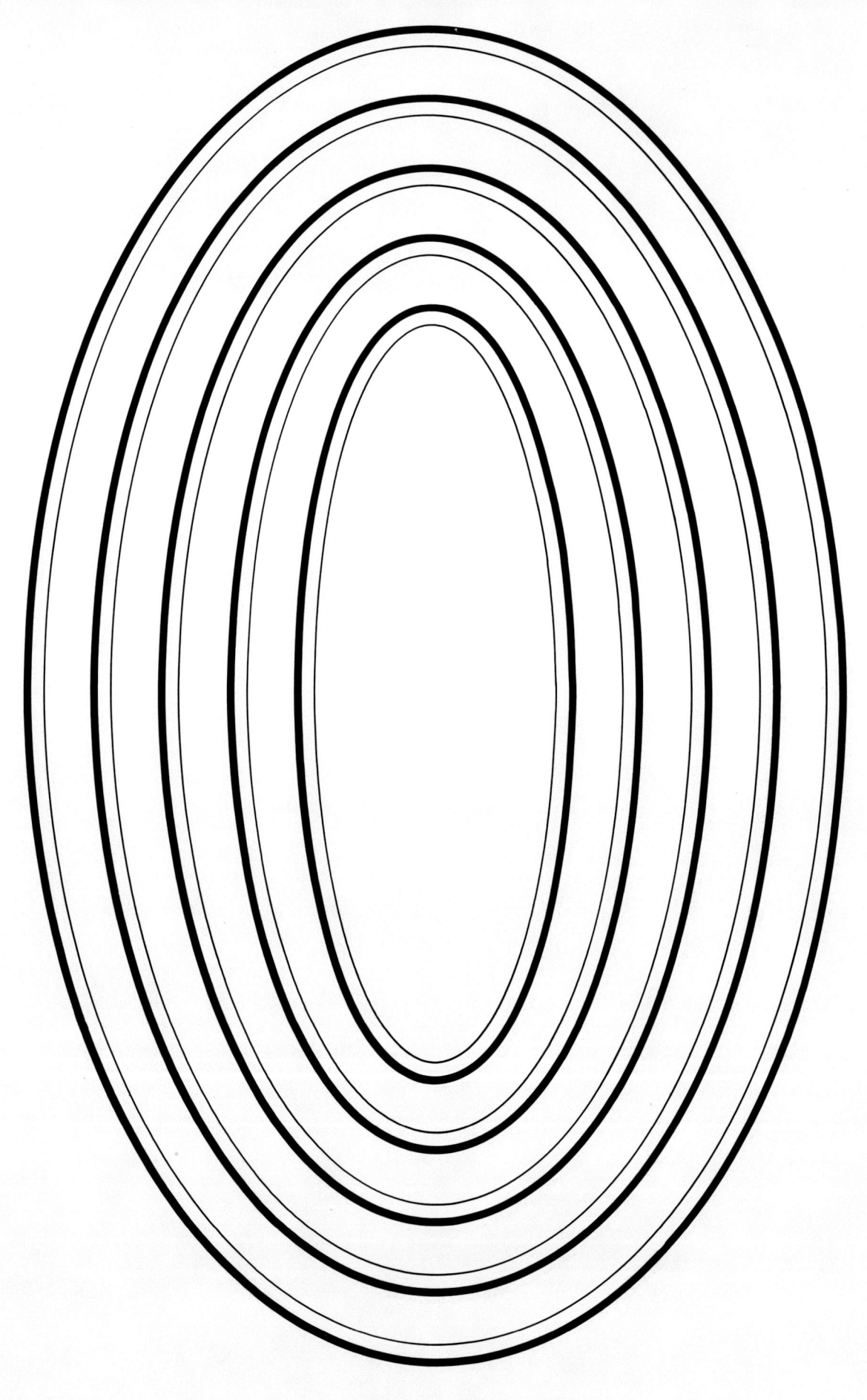

The ovals on plates 14–26 can be nested.

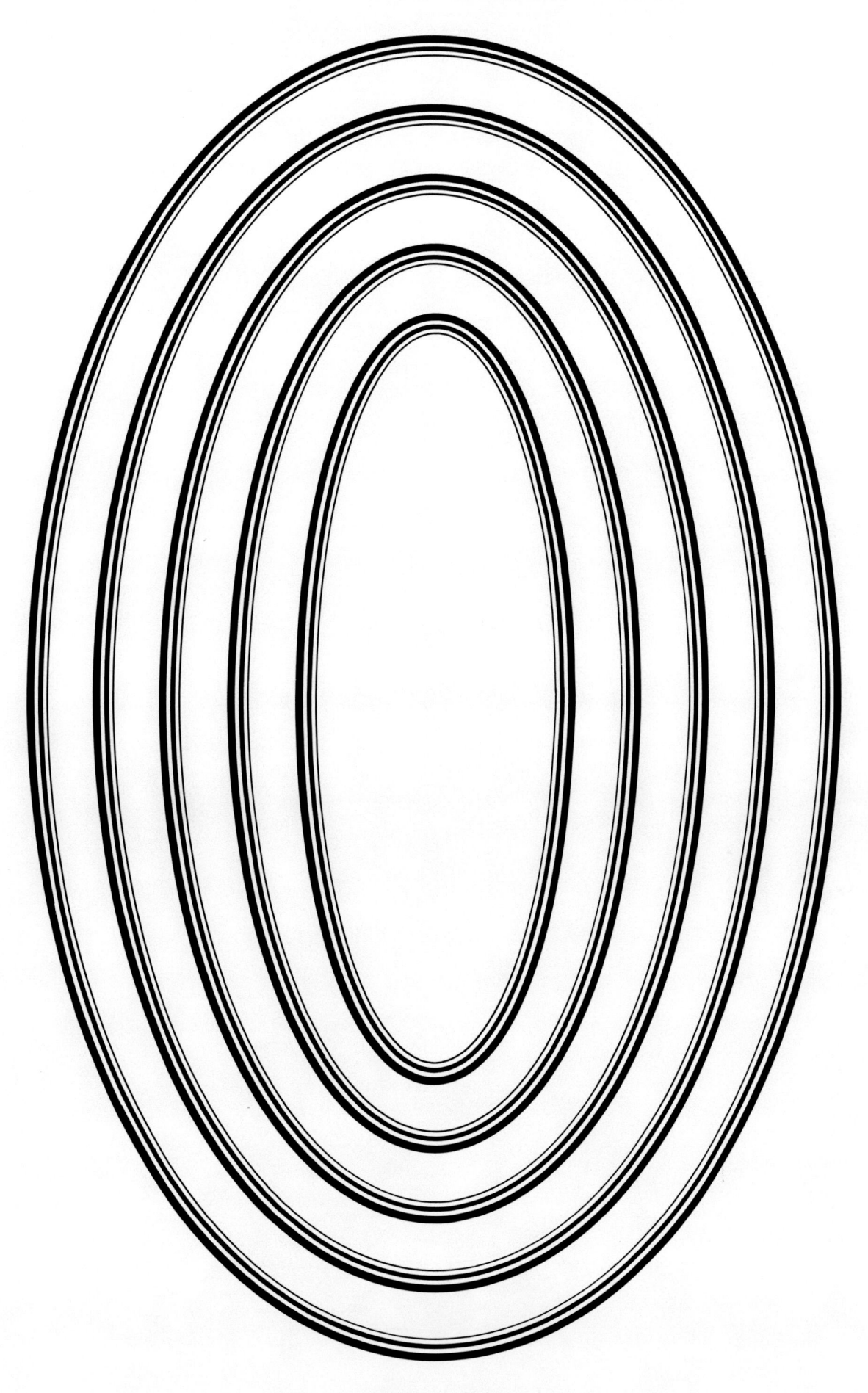

The ovals on plates 14–26 can be nested.

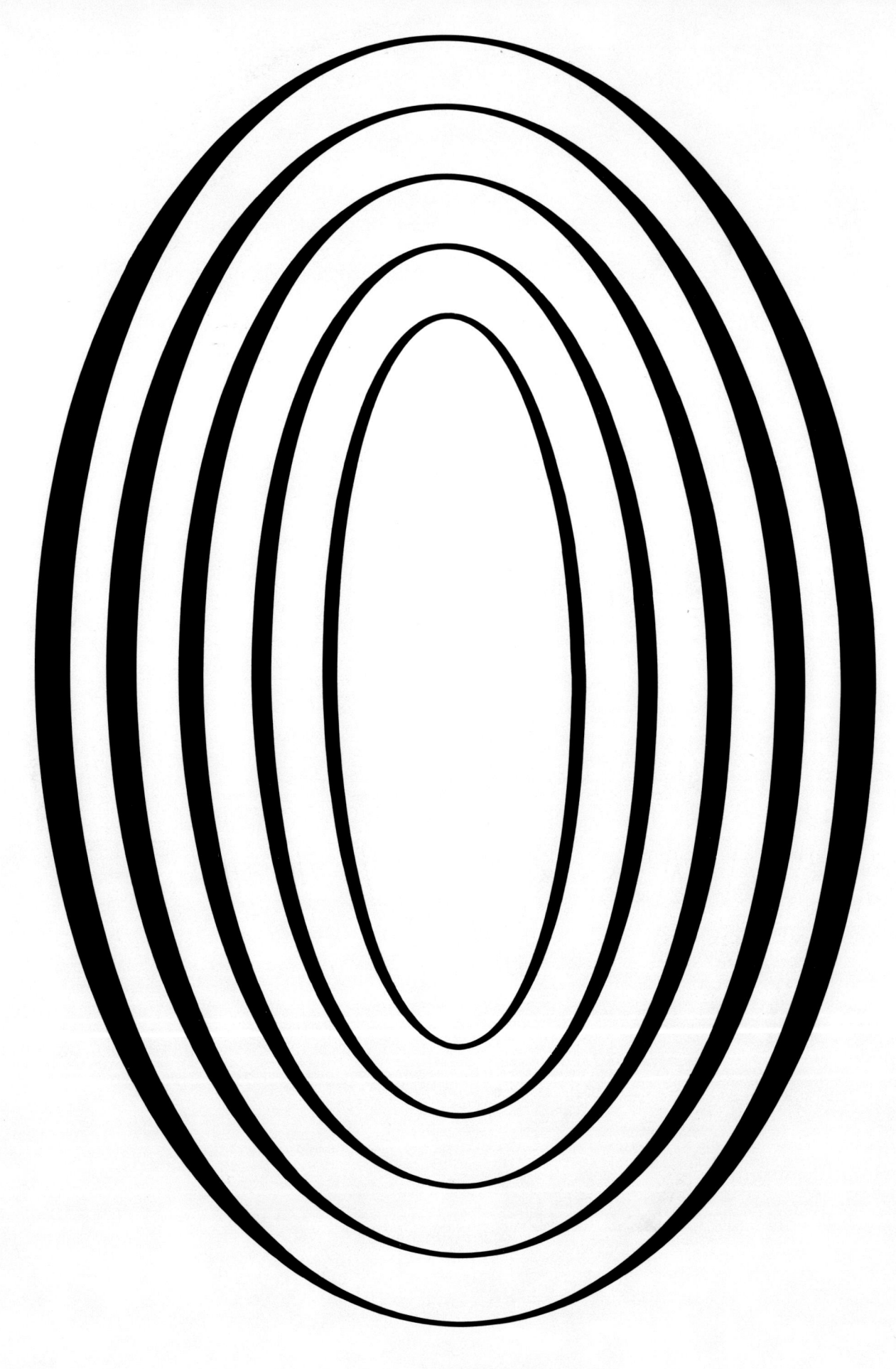

The ovals on plates 14–26 can be nested.

The ovals on plates 14–26 can be nested.

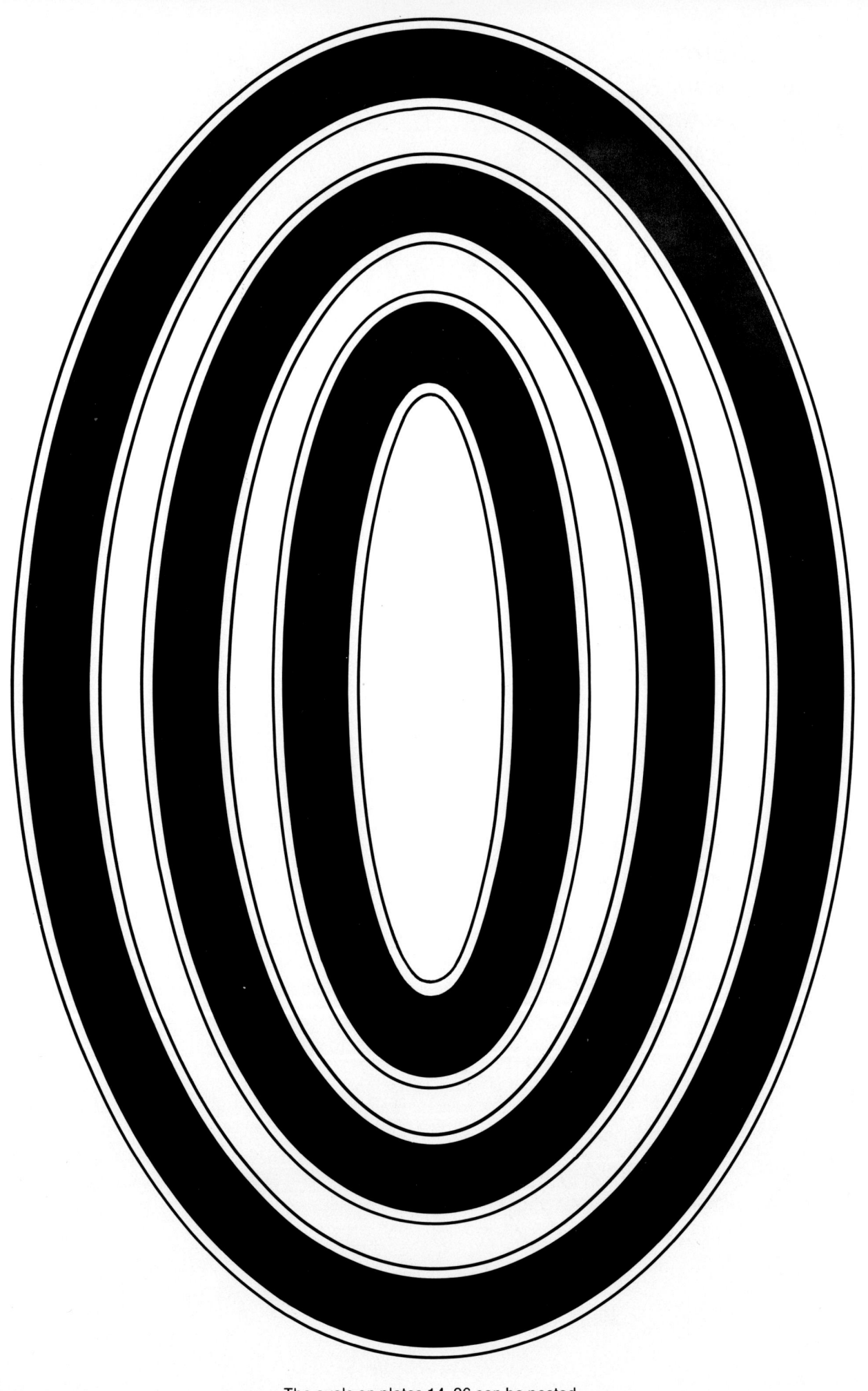

The ovals on plates 14–26 can be nested.

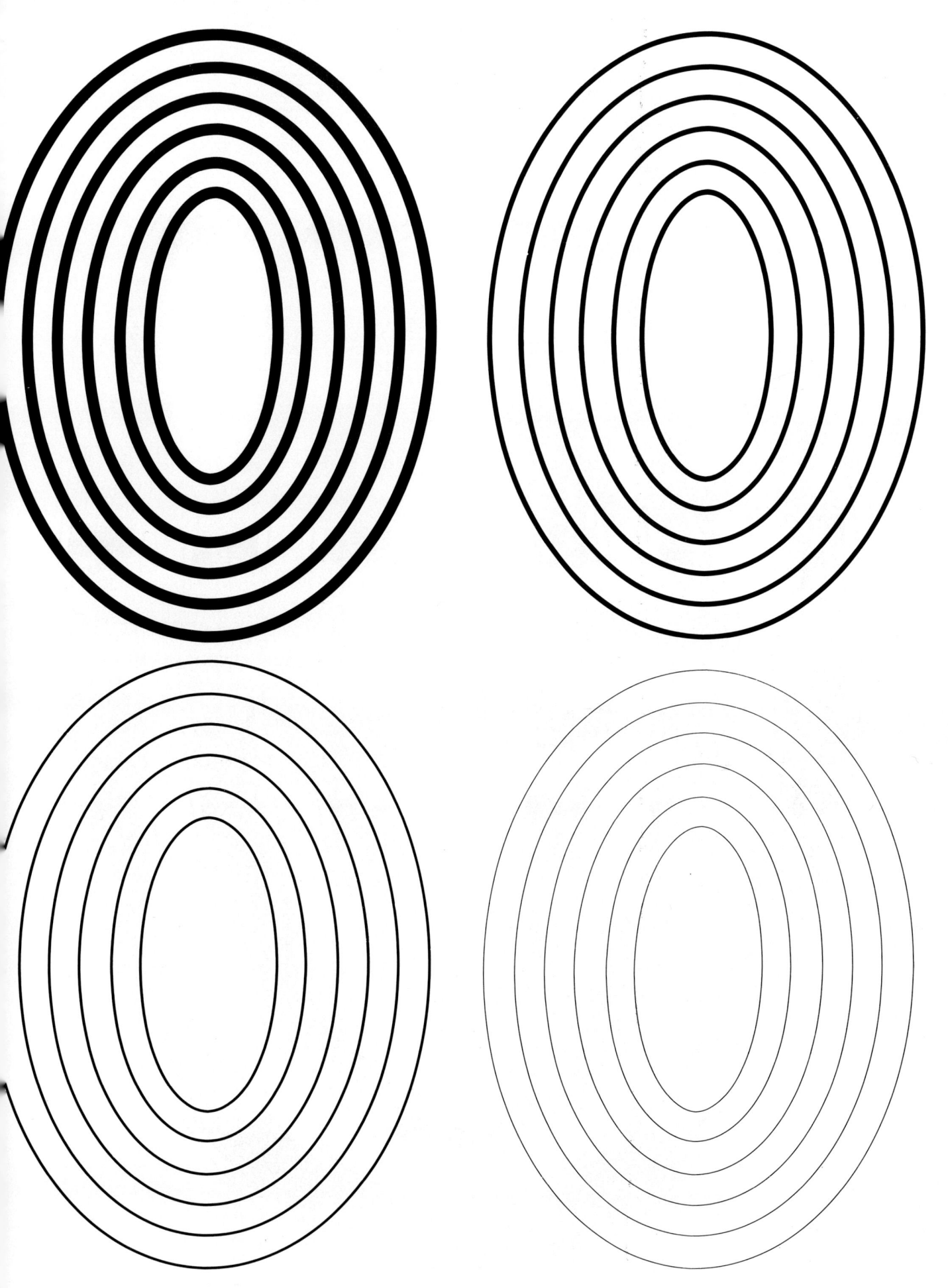

The ovals on plates 27–29 can be nested.

The ovals on plates 27–29 can be nested.

The ovals on plates 27–29 can be nested.

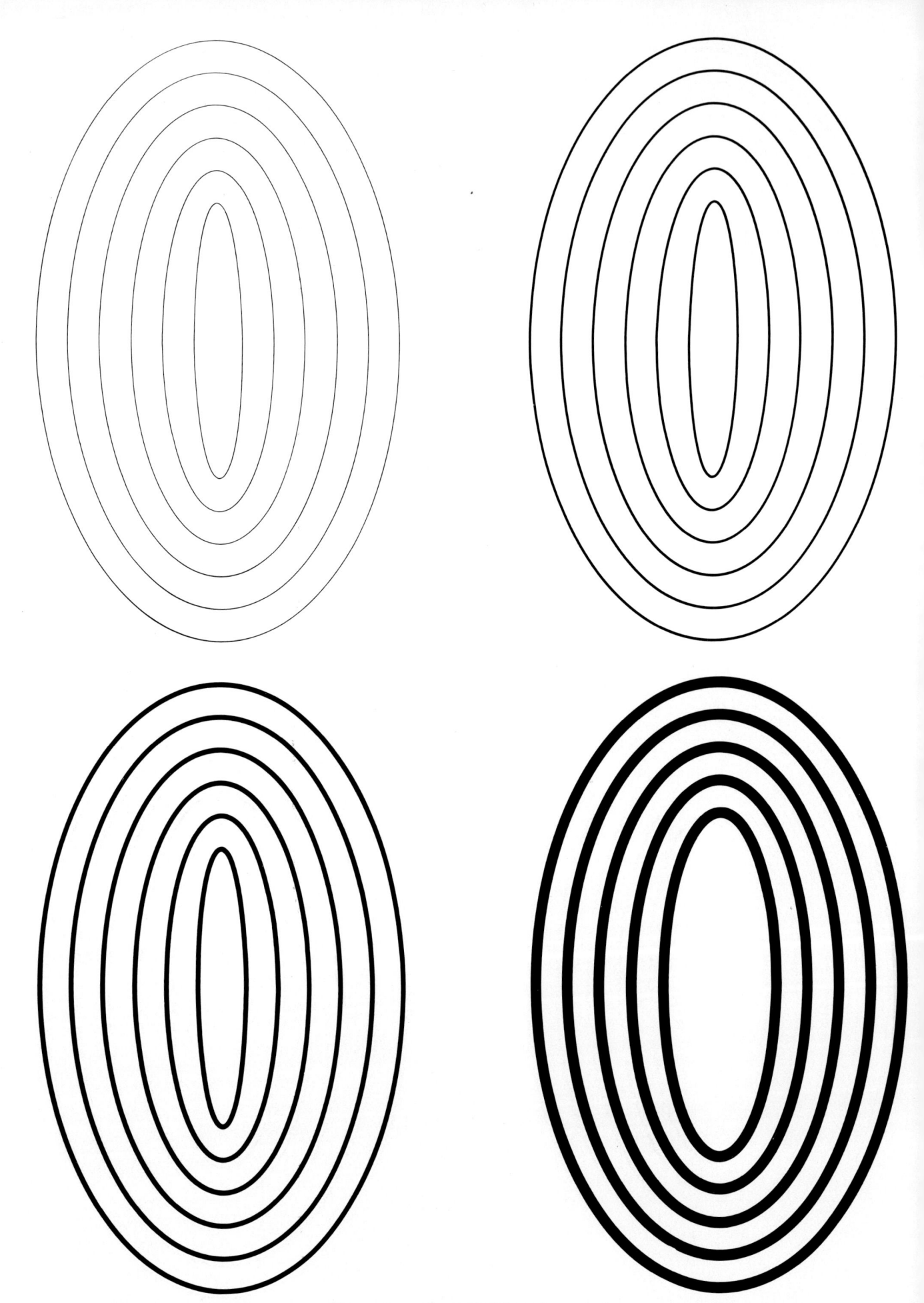

The ovals on plates 30–32 can be nested.

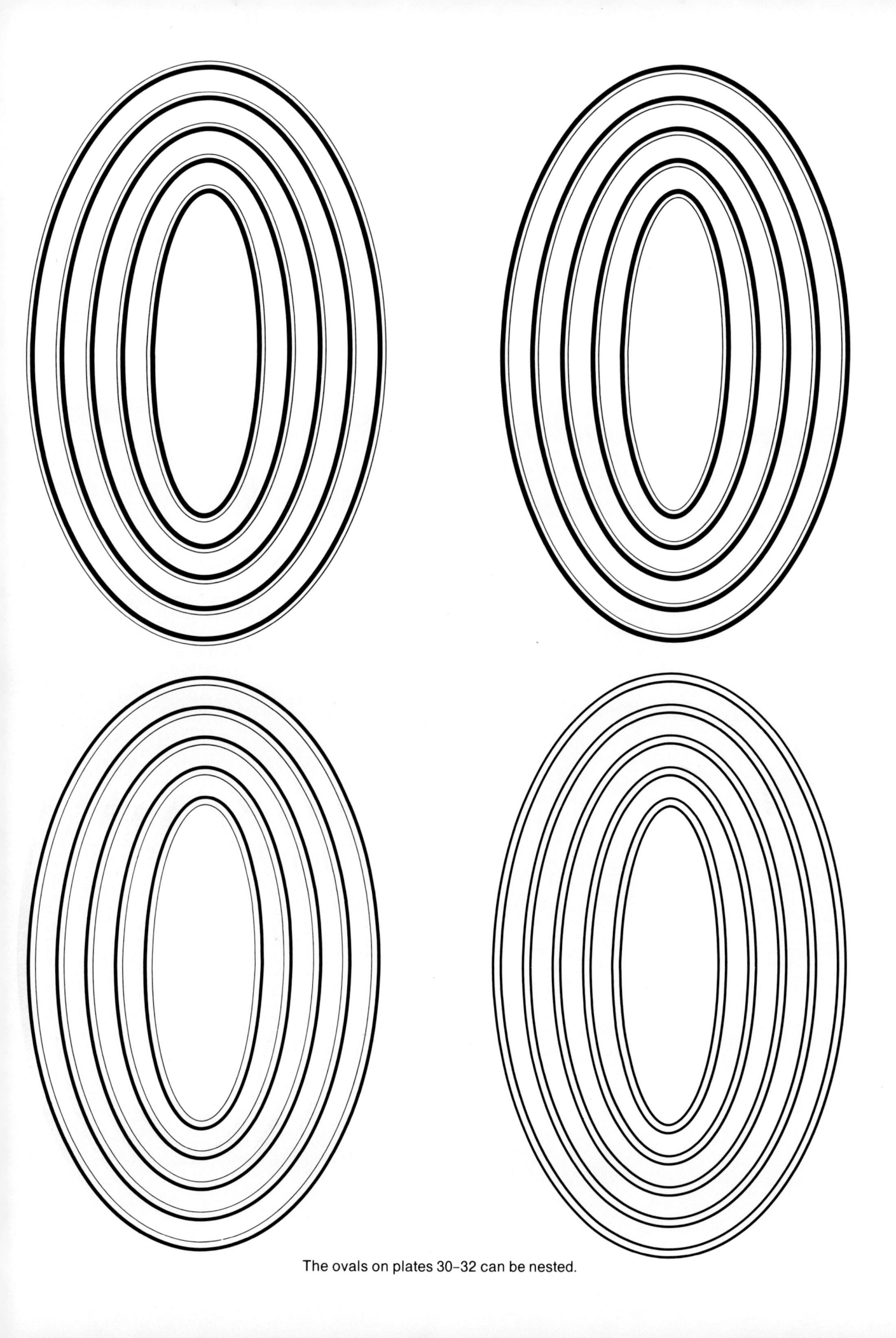

The ovals on plates 30–32 can be nested.

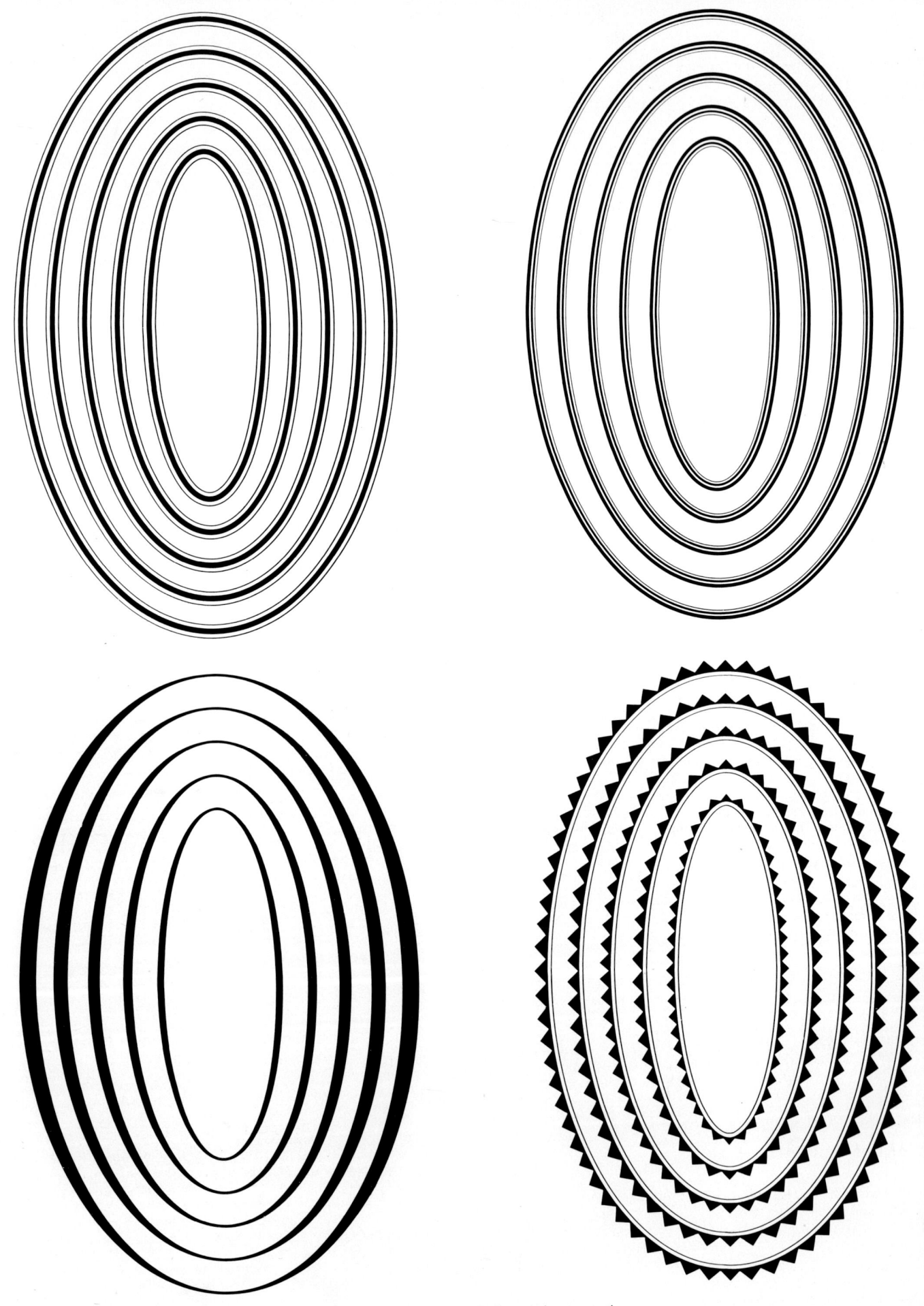

The ovals on plates 30–32 can be nested.